PIANO • VOCAL • GUITAR

# OPEN HEAVEN / *River Wild*

T0066163

ISBN 978-1-4950-5940-7

HAL•LEONARD®
CORPORATION
7777 W. BLUEMOUND RD. P.O. BOX 13819 MILWAUKEE, WI 53213

In Australia Contact:
**Hal Leonard Australia Pty. Ltd.**
4 Lentara Court
Cheltenham, Victoria, 3192 Australia
Email: ausadmin@halleonard.com.au

Visit Hal Leonard Online at
**www.halleonard.com**

# O PRAISE THE NAME

## (Anástasis)

Words and Music by MARTY SAMPSON,
BENJAMIN HASTINGS and DEAN USSHER

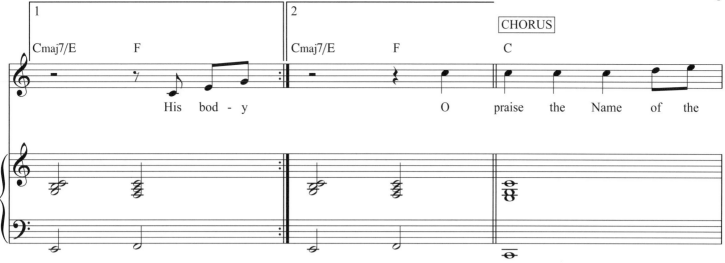

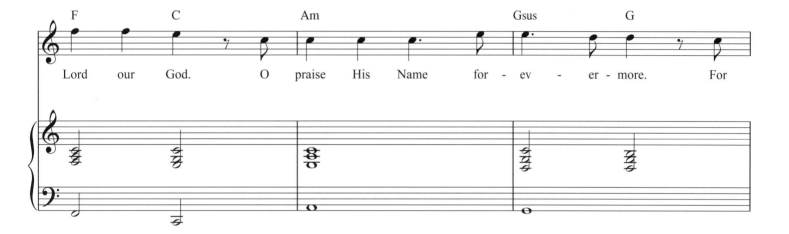

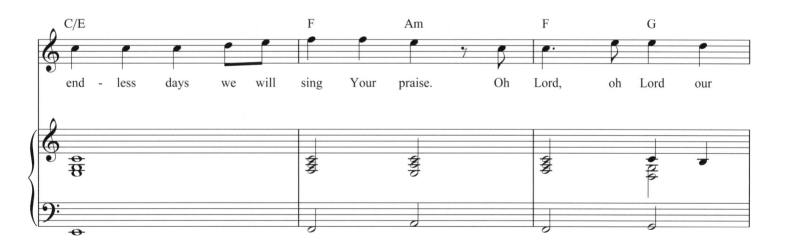

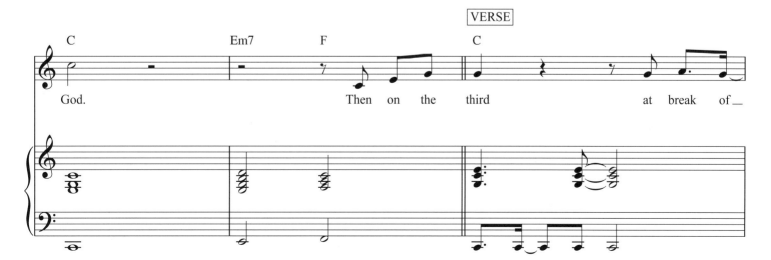

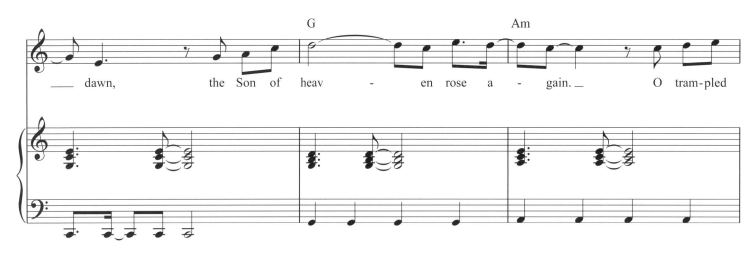

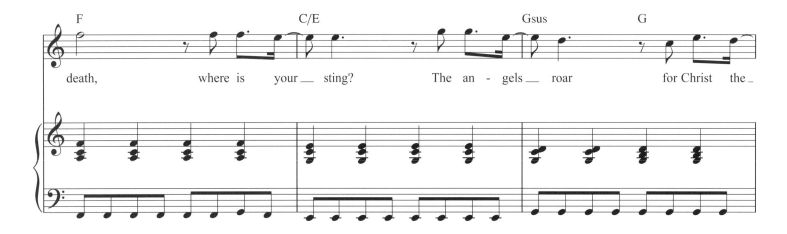

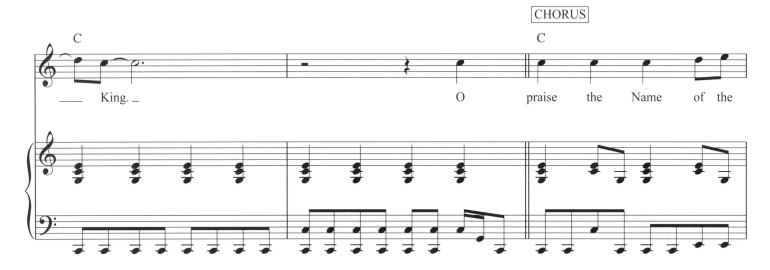

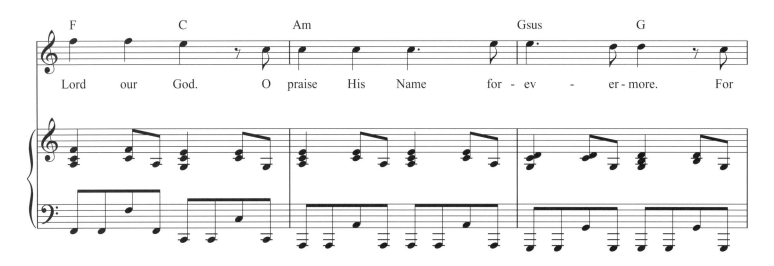

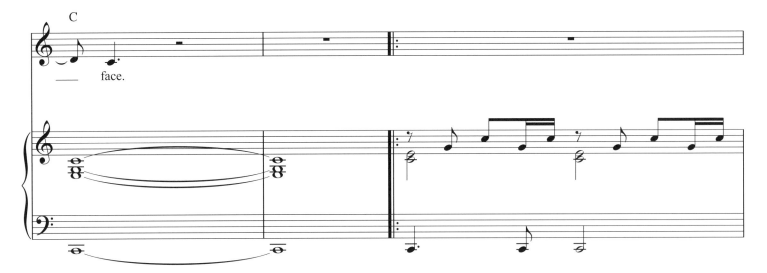

face.

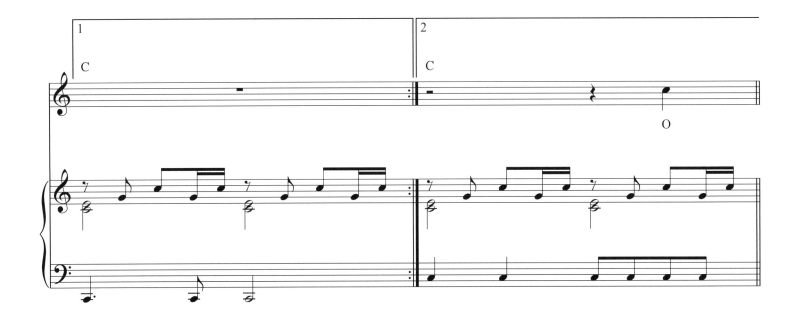

O

CHORUS

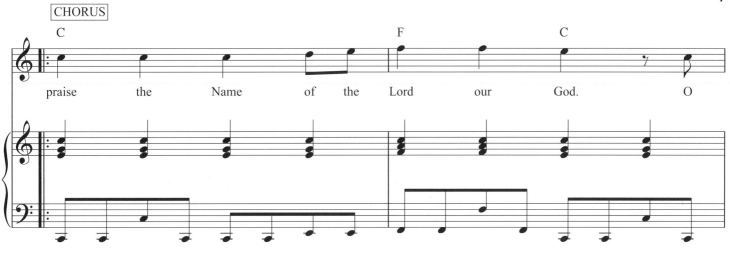

praise the Name of the Lord our God. O

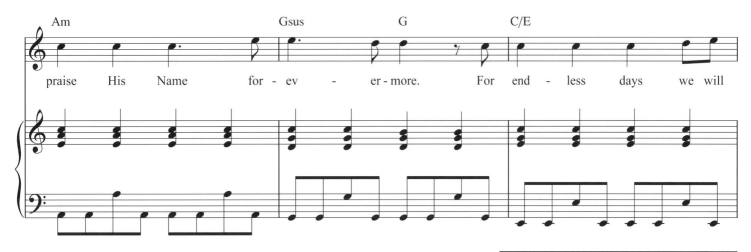

praise His Name for - ev - er - more. For end - less days we will

sing Your praise. Oh Lord, oh Lord our God. O

**2**

God. Oh Lord, oh Lord our God.

# LOVE ON THE LINE

Words and Music by ARYEL MURPHY,
SCOTT LIGERTWOOD and BROOKE LIGERTWOOD

**With momentum** ♪ = 172

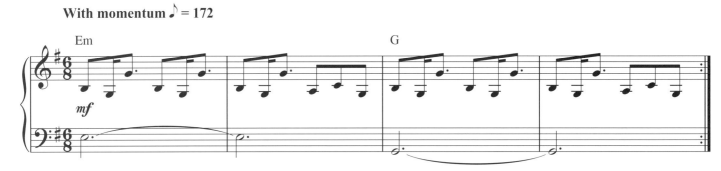

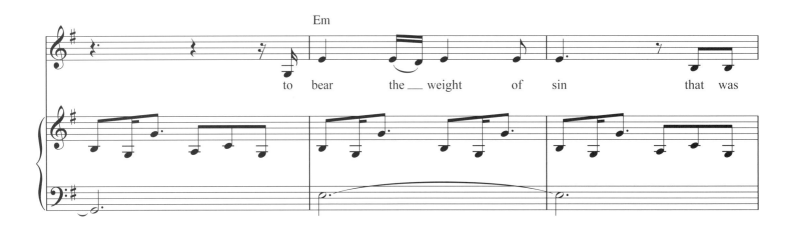

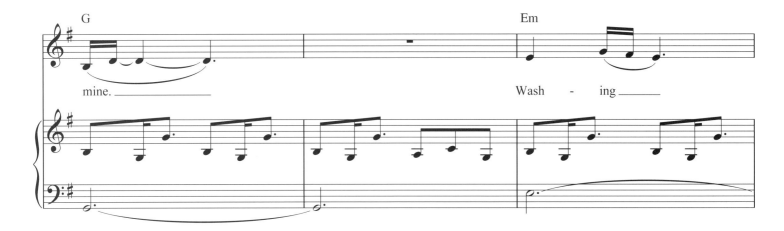

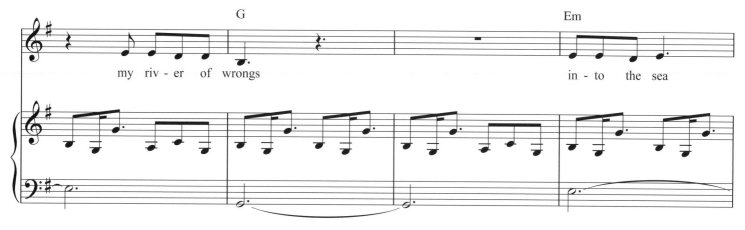

CHORUS

God, my Sav - iour.

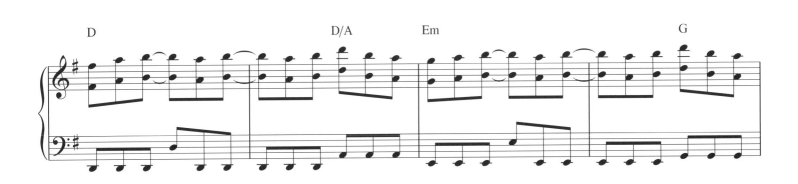

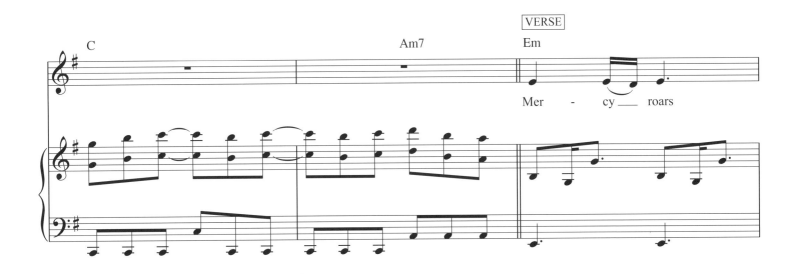

VERSE

Mer - cy ___ roars

like hur - ri - cane ___ winds.

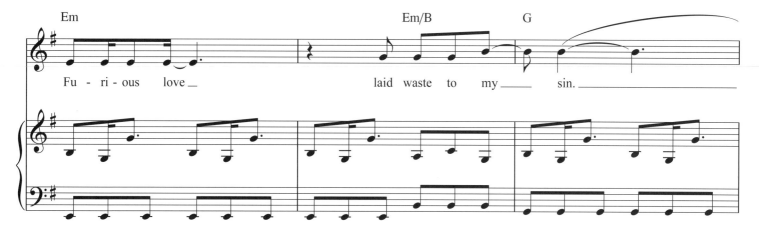

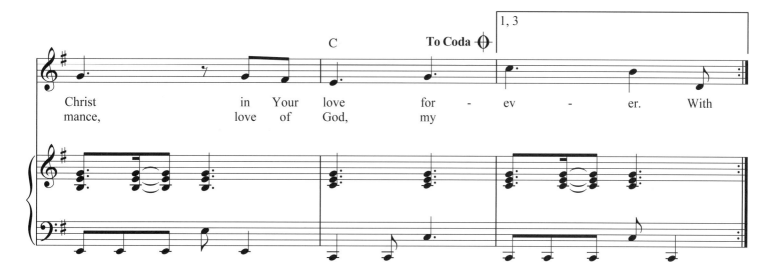

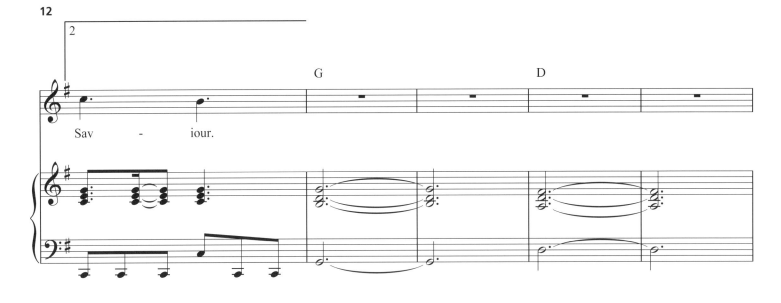

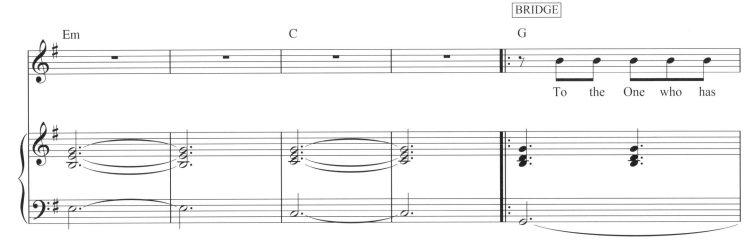

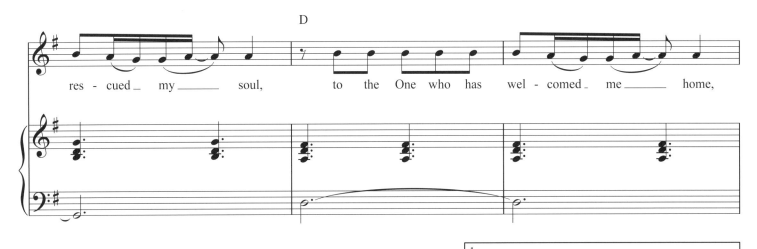

sing for - ev - er. ____

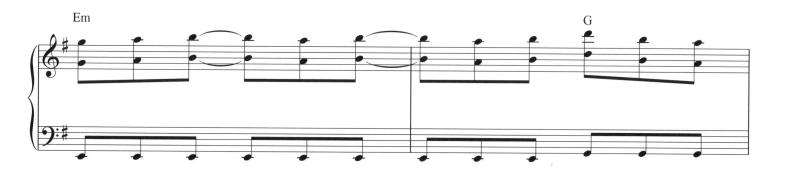

With

**CODA**

BRIDGE

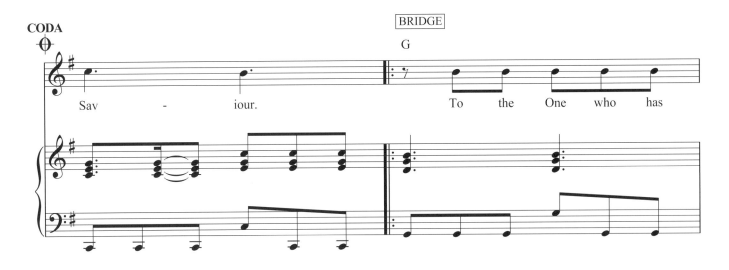

Sav - iour. To the One who has

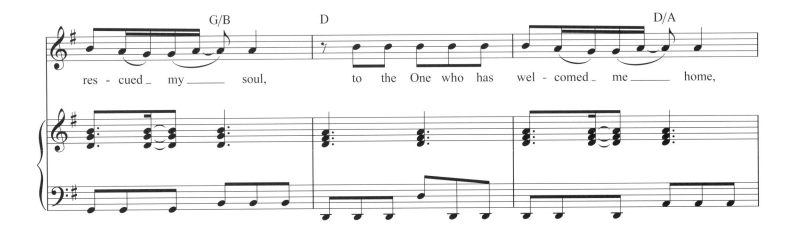

res - cued _ my _____ soul, to the One who has wel - comed _ me _____ home,

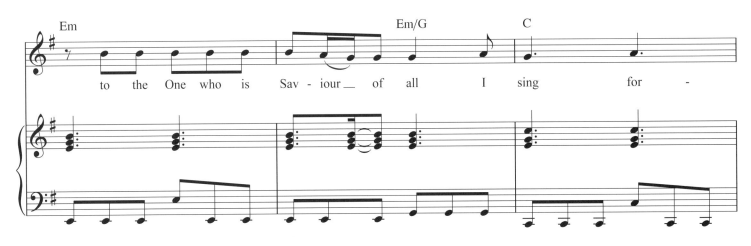

to the One who is Sav - iour _ of all I sing for -

1. ev - er. 2. ev - er.

# ONE THING

Words and Music by JOEL HOUSTON,
AODHAN KING and DYLAN THOMAS

Slowly ♩ = 56

VERSE

I tast - ed the world, seen more than e - nough its prom - is - es fleet - ing.
Just one thing I ask and this I will seek, if on - ly to know You.

Of wa - ter and wine, I emp - tied the cup and found _ my - self want - ing.
To be where You are and go where You lead, my God, _ I will fol - low.

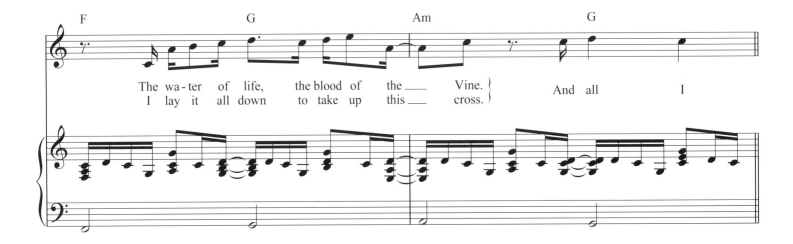

CHORUS

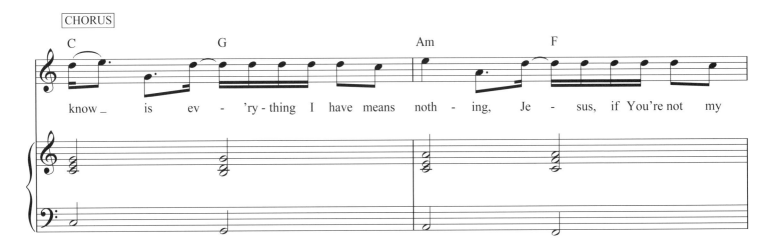

now.     And all ___ I    want ___ is ev - 'ry-thing You are and

noth - ing, Je - sus, if You're not my  one ___ thing, ev - 'ry-thing to me right

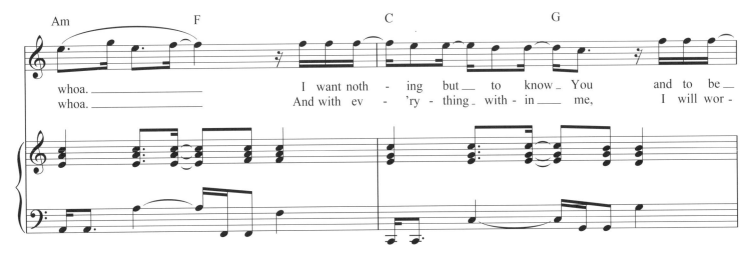

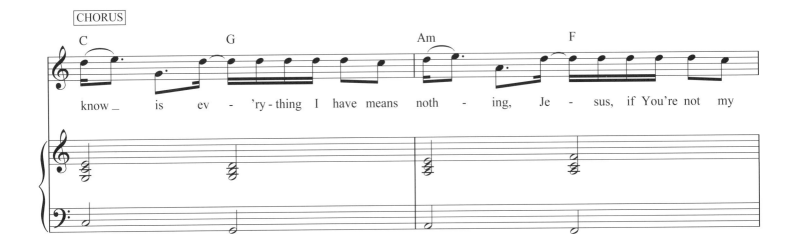

one ___ thing, ev - 'ry - thing I need right now. All ___ I need is You right

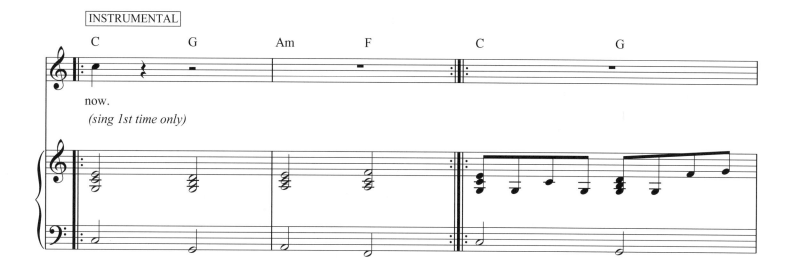

INSTRUMENTAL

now.

*(sing 1st time only)*

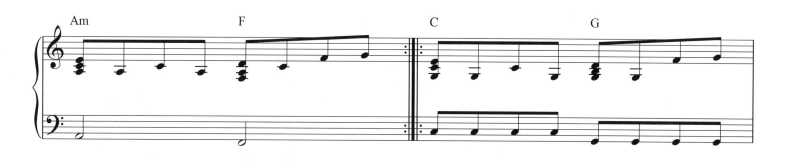

1

2

And all ___ I

CHORUS

| C | | G | | Am | | F | |

know  is  ev - 'ry-thing I have means noth - ing, Je - sus, if You're not my
want  is  ev - 'ry-thing You are and noth - ing, Je - sus, if You're not my

**1**

| C | | G | | Am | | F | |

one  thing,  ev - 'ry-thing I need right now.  And all ___ I
one  thing,  ev - 'ry-thing to me right

**2**

BRIDGE

| Am | | F | | C | | G | |

now.  And I'll ___ sing:  Whoa, _____
Whoa, _____

| Am | | F | | C | | G | |

whoa. _____  I want noth - ing but ___ to know ___ You  and to be ___
whoa. _____  And with ev - 'ry - thing ___ with - in ___ me,  I will wor -

# OPEN HEAVEN
## (River Wild)

Words and Music by MATT CROCKER
and MARTY SAMPSON

**Moderate Ballad** ♩ = 69

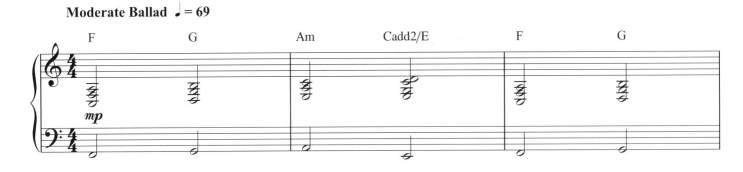

Signs and won-ders from __ a-

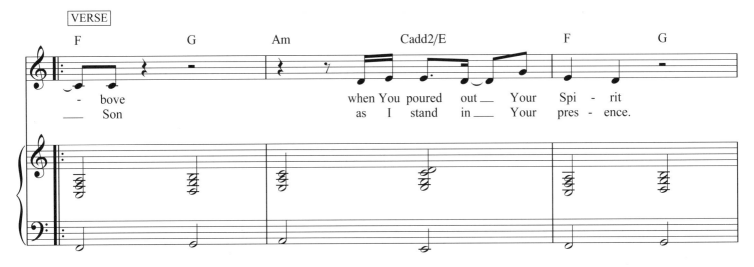

VERSE

-bove ___ Son

when You poured out __ Your Spi-rit
as I stand in __ Your pres-ence.

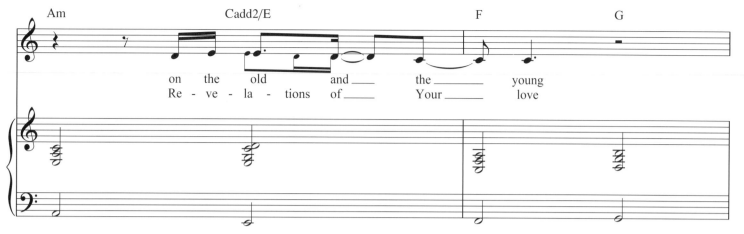

on the old and \_\_\_\_ the _____ young
Re - ve - la - tions of \_\_\_\_\_ Your _____ love

in the pow'r of \_\_\_\_\_ Your pres - ence.
as I look to \_\_\_\_\_ the heav - ens.

**CHORUS**

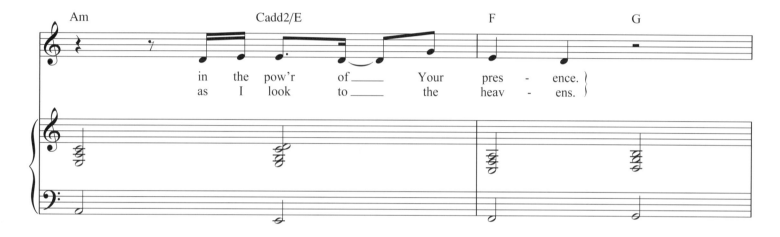

Ho - ly Spi - rit rain, fall - ing like a \_\_\_\_ flood. Break up - on my

praise as I sing of \_\_\_ Your \_\_\_ love. Ho - ly Spi - rit fire, burn with - in my \_

soul as I call on __ Your __ Name, as I call on __ Your __

__ Name.

Dreams and vi-sions of __ the __

as I call on __ Your __ Name, as I call on __ Your __

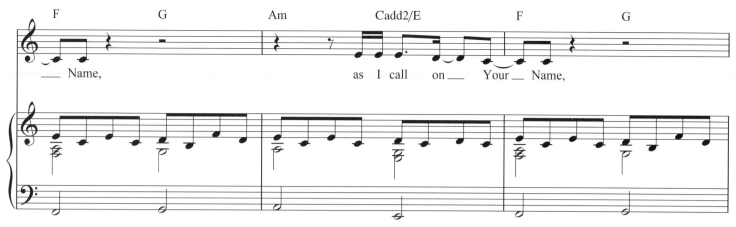

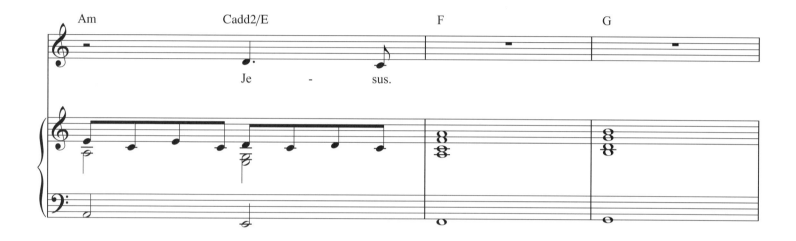

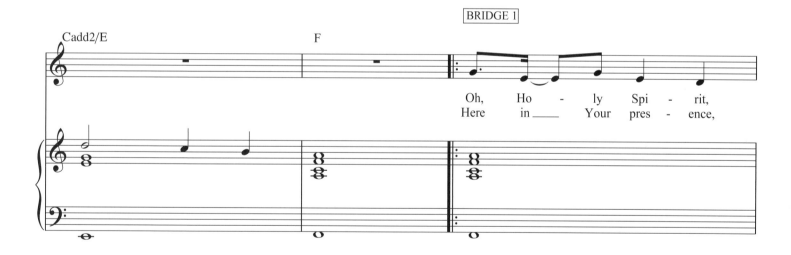

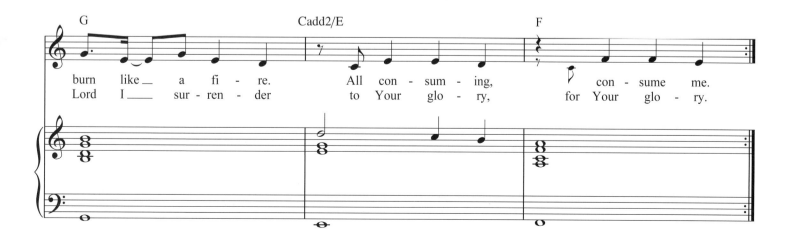

26

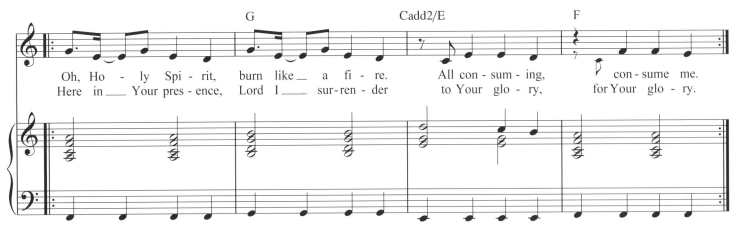

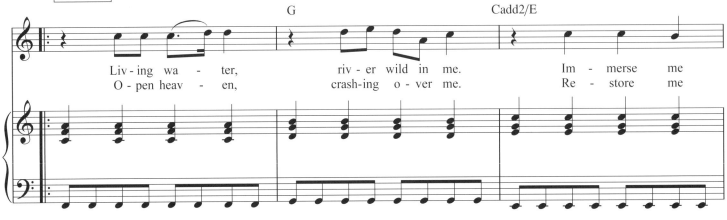

BRIDGE 2

BRIDGE 1

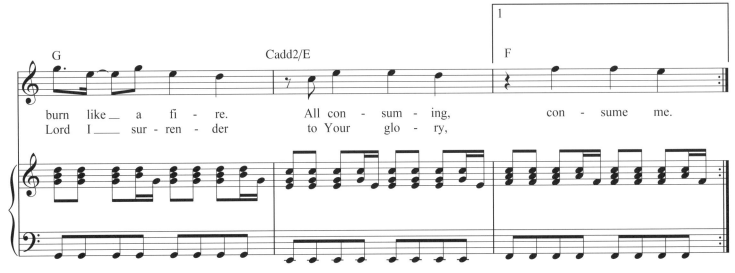

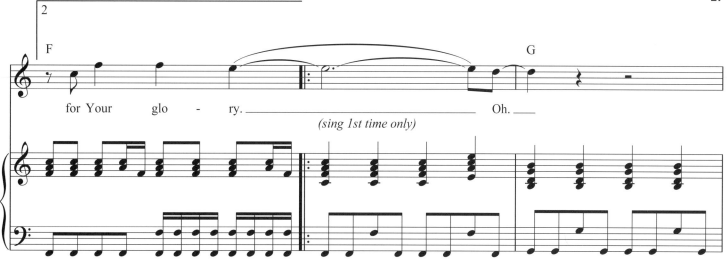

*(sing 1st time only)*

for Your glo - ry. _____ Oh. ___

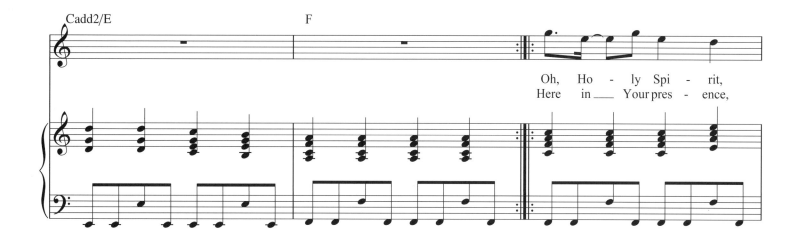

Oh, Ho - ly Spi - rit,
Here in ___ Your pres - ence,

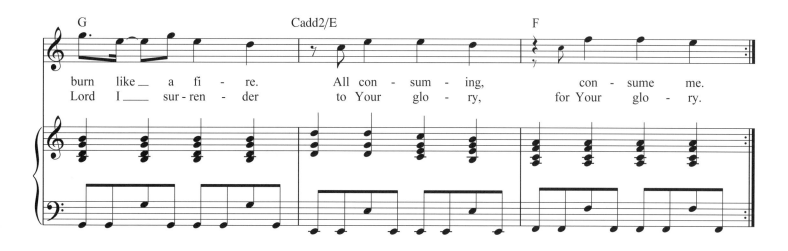

burn like ___ a fi - re. All con - sum - ing, con - sume me.
Lord I ___ sur - ren - der to Your glo - ry, for Your glo - ry.

CHORUS

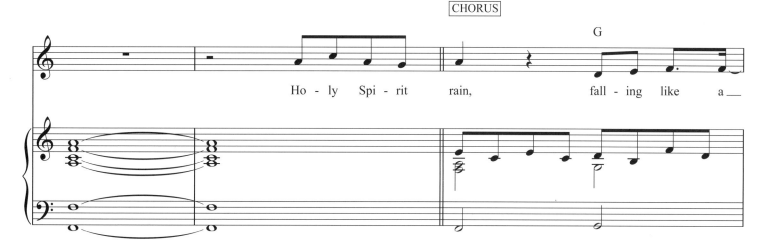

Ho - ly Spi - rit rain, fall - ing like a ___

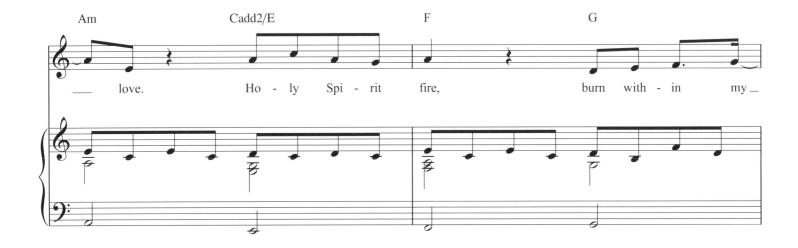

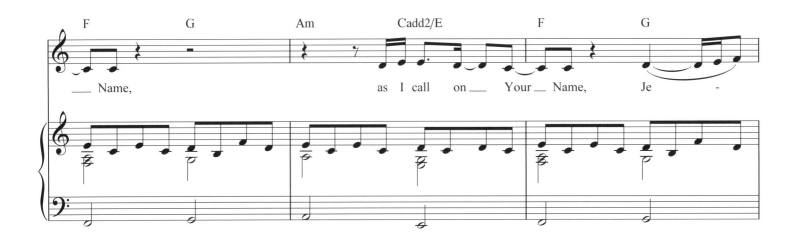

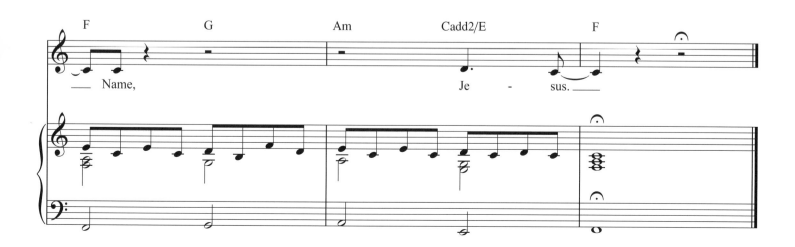

# TRANSFIGURATION

Words and Music by AODHAN KING,
BROOKE LIGERTWOOD, SCOTT LIGERTWOOD
and TAYA SMITH

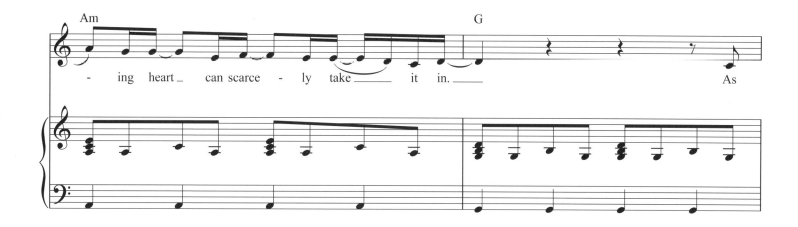

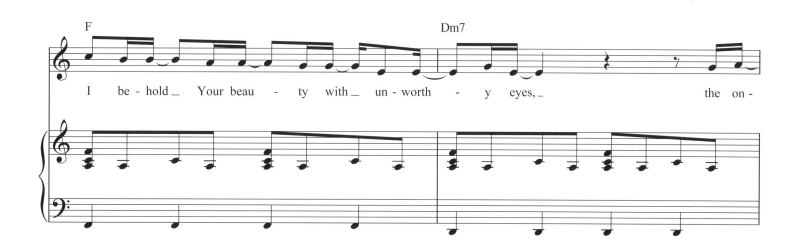

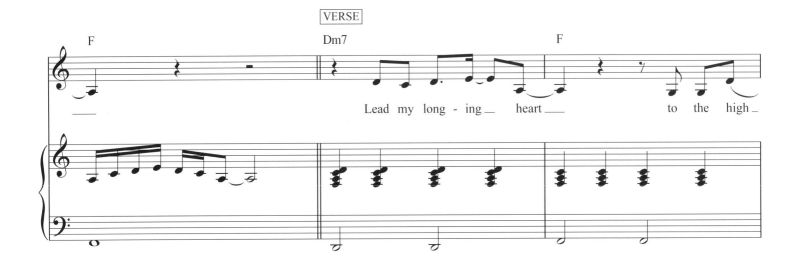

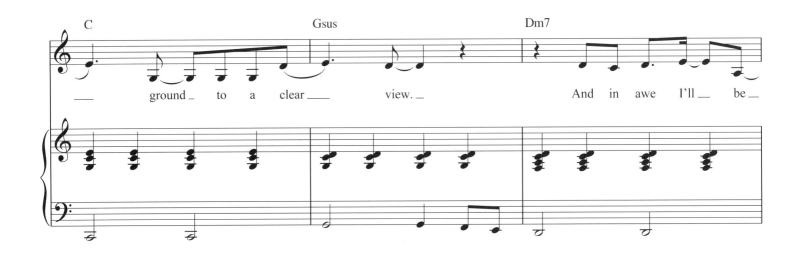

**CODA**

Hal - le - lu - jah, \_\_ hal - le - lu -

\- jah, \_\_ hal - le - lu - jah \_\_ my King. \_\_

Now I know \_

BRIDGE

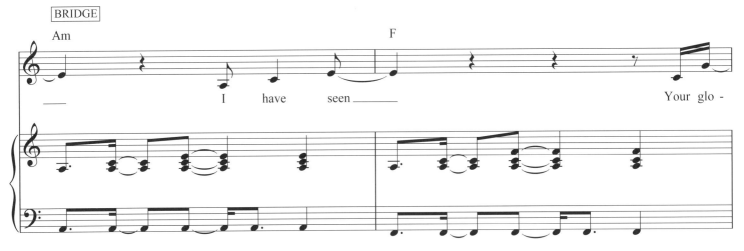

I have seen _____ Your glo -

- ry that ___ can-not ___ be un - seen. _____ I am changed _

___ and chang - ing still _____ as I look _

___ up - on ___ You, Lord, ___ and ___ be - lieve. _____

CHORUS

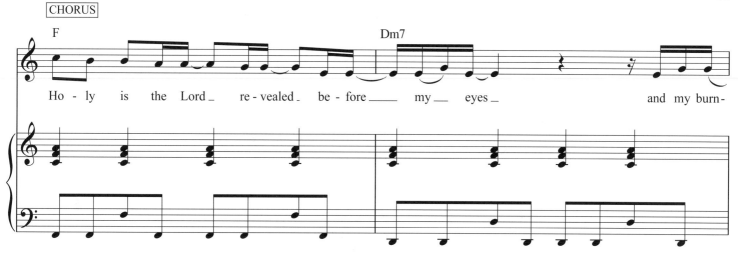

Ho - ly is the Lord _ re - vealed _ be - fore _ my _ eyes _ and my burn-

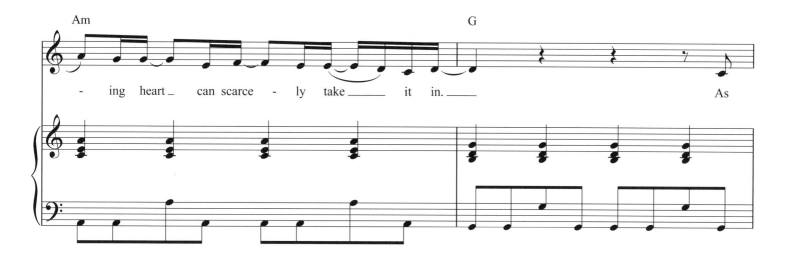

- ing heart _ can scarce - ly take _ it in. _ As

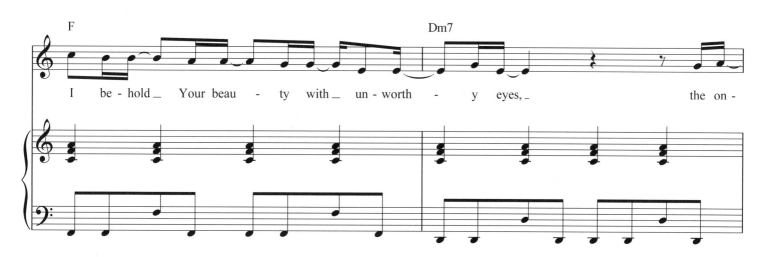

I be - hold _ Your beau - ty with _ un - worth - y eyes, _ the on -

- ly song _ my soul _ can find _ to sing _ is hal - le - lu -

*(cued notes: opt. lead vocal)*

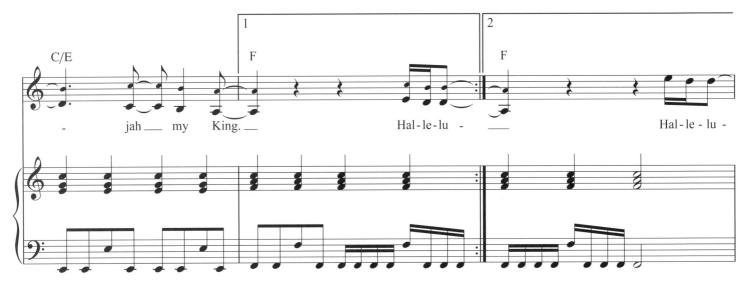

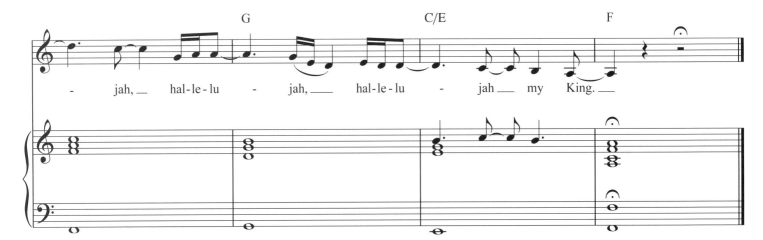

# WHAT A SAVIOUR

Words and Music by CHRIS DAVENPORT
and JOEL HOUSTON

CHORUS

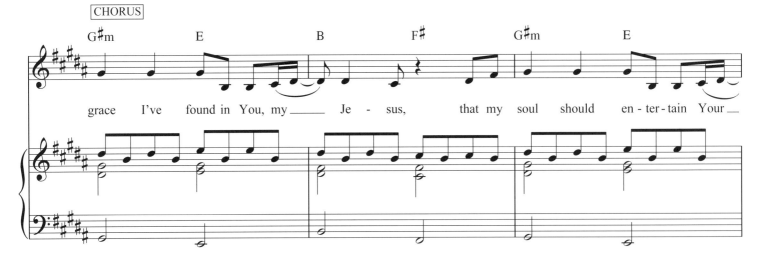

grace I've found in You, my _____ Je - sus, that my soul should en - ter - tain Your _____

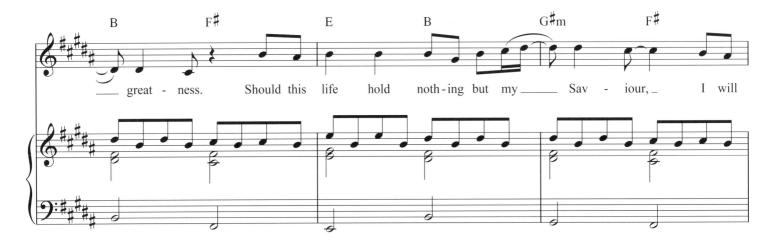

_____ great - ness. Should this life hold noth - ing but my _____ Sav - iour, _____ I will

praise You al - ways. _____ Oh, _____

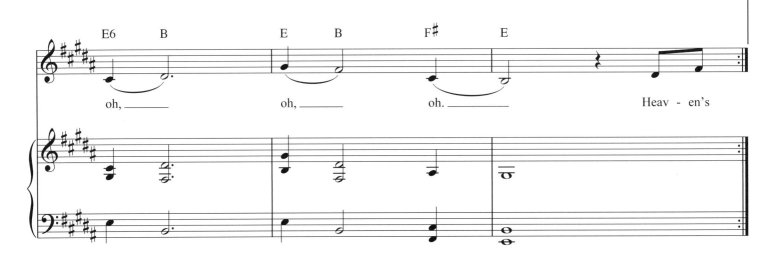

oh, _____ oh, _____ oh. _____ Heav - en's

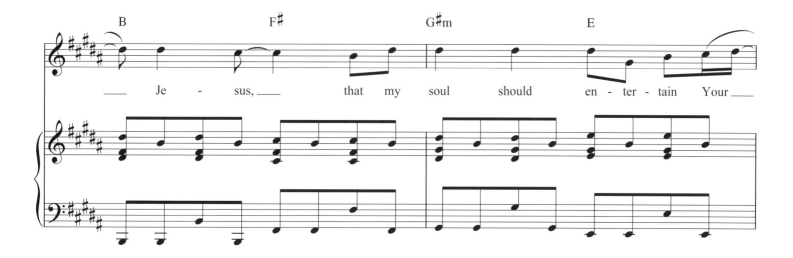

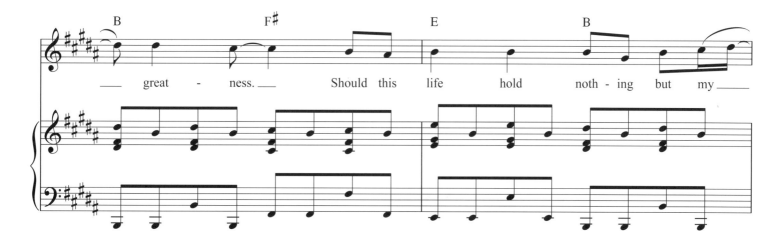

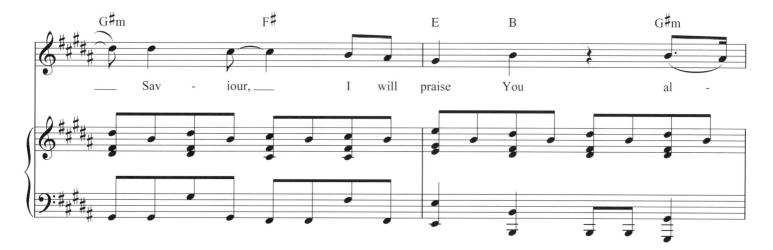

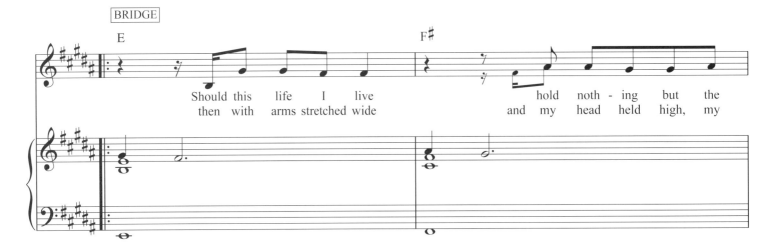

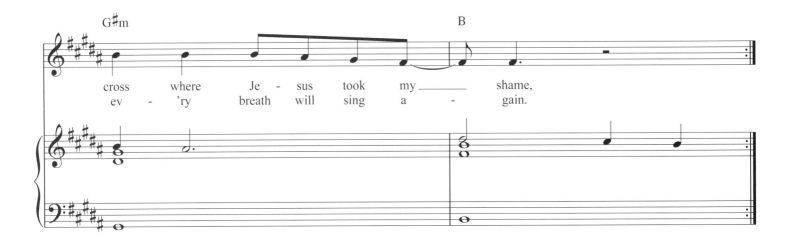

CHORUS

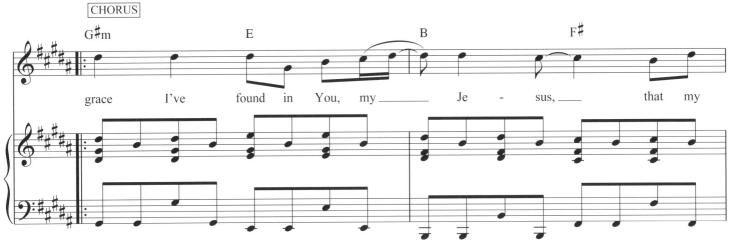

grace I've found in You, my _____ Je - sus, _____ that my

soul should en - ter - tain Your _____ great - ness. _____ Should this

life hold noth - ing but my _____ Sav - iour, _____ I will

praise You al - ways. Oh what

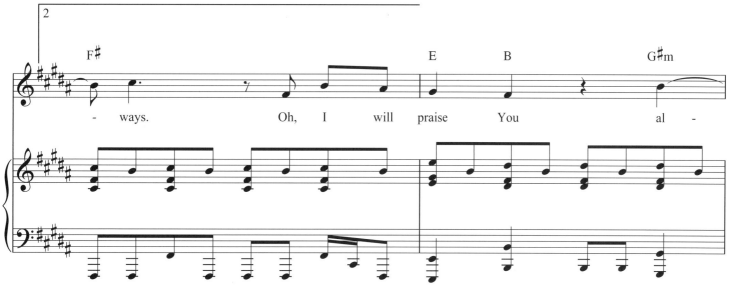

-ways. Oh, I will praise You al -

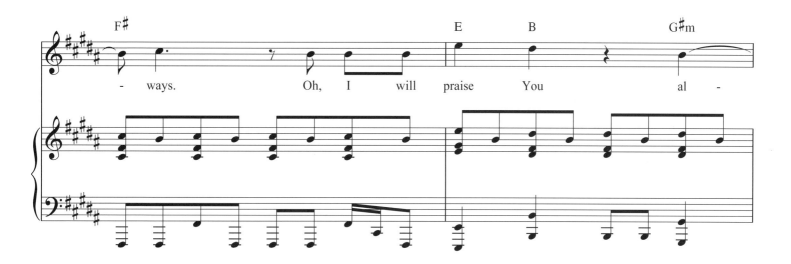

-ways. Oh, I will praise You al -

-ways. I will praise You al - ways. _____

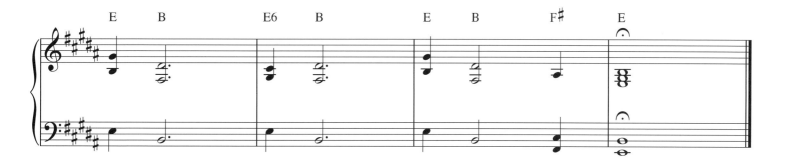

# HEART LIKE HEAVEN

Words and Music by JOEL HOUSTON
and MATT CROCKER

**With constant motion** ♩ = 69

VERSE

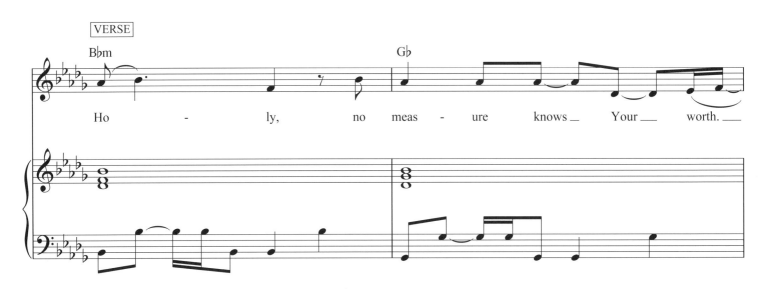

Ho - ly, no meas - ure knows Your worth.

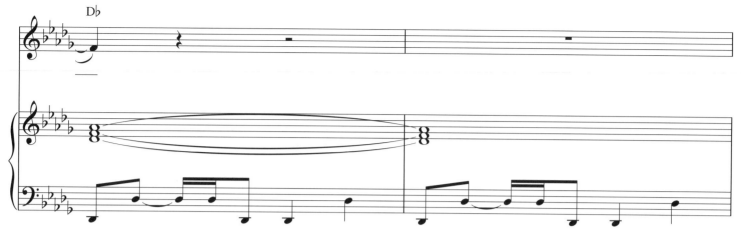

Face ___ down, where mer - cy finds ___ me ___ first. ___

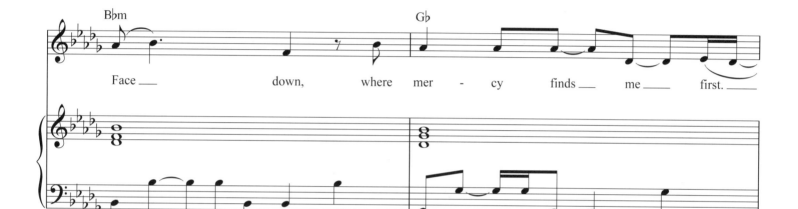

Oh, _____
Oh, _____

if You sought per - fec - tion, oh, _____
and I'll throw my weak - ness, oh, _____

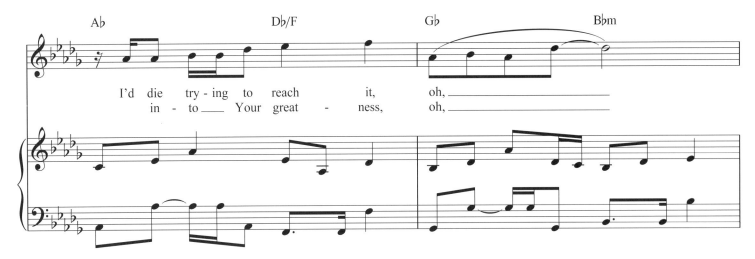

I'd die try-ing to reach it, oh, _____
in - to ___ Your great - ness, oh, _____

but this bro-ken heart is all _____ You want. __
if this bro-ken heart is all _____ You want. __

CHORUS

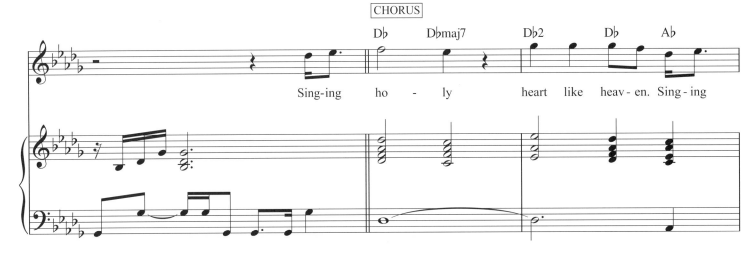

Sing-ing ho - ly heart like heav - en. Sing-ing

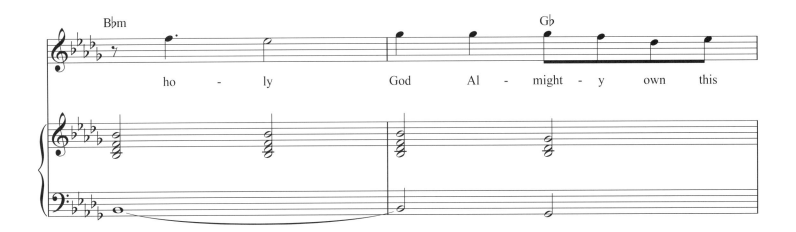

ho - ly God Al - might - y own this

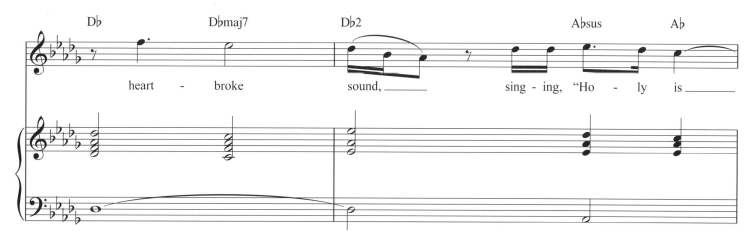

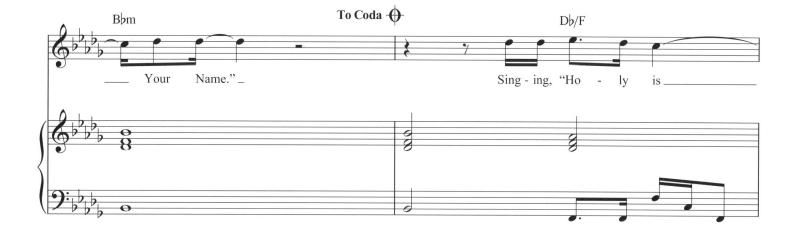

**CODA**

CHORUS

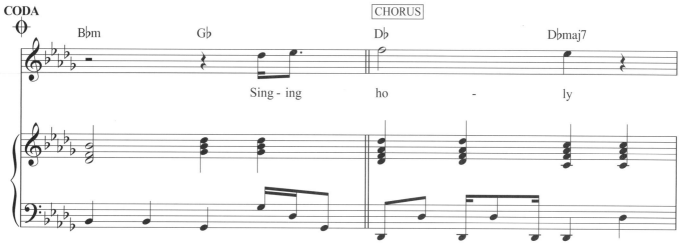

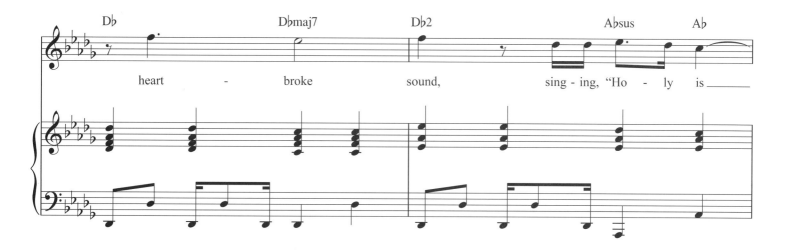

Your Name."

You're wor - thy of ___ all praise. _

___ You're wor - thy of ___ all praise. _____

For You are

# JESUS I NEED YOU

Words and Music by REUBEN MORGAN,
BROOKE LIGERTWOOD, SCOTT LIGERTWOOD
and JARRED ROGERS

**Worship Ballad** ♩ = 78

CHORUS

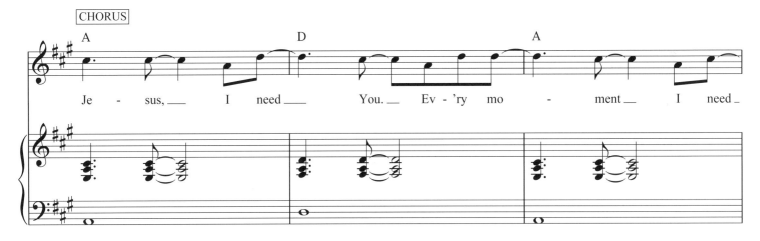

Je - sus, __ I need __ You. __ Ev - 'ry mo - ment __ I need __

__ You. __ Hear now __ this grace - bought heart __ sing out __

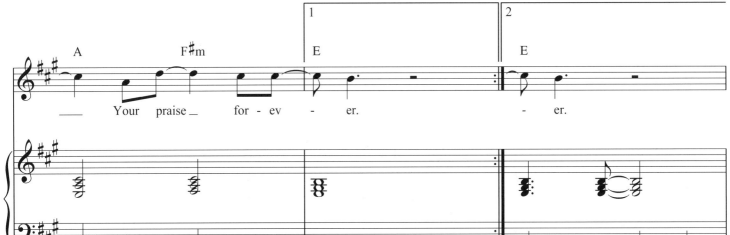

__ Your praise __ for - ev - er.  - er.

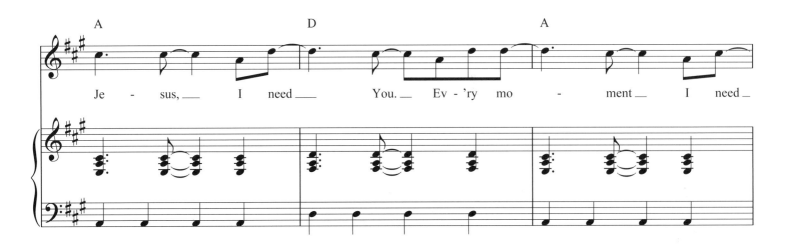

Je - sus, __ I need __ You. __ Ev - 'ry mo - ment __ I need __

You. Hear ___ now ___ this grace - bought heart ___ sing out ___

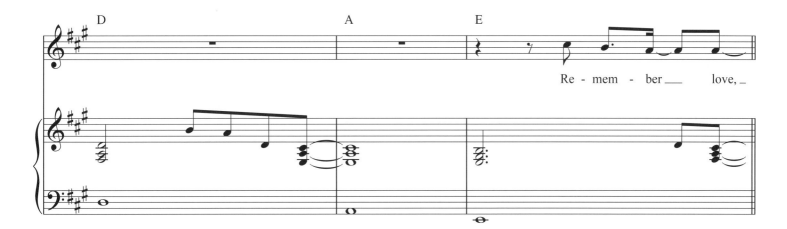

Your praise ___ for - ev - er. Oh. ___

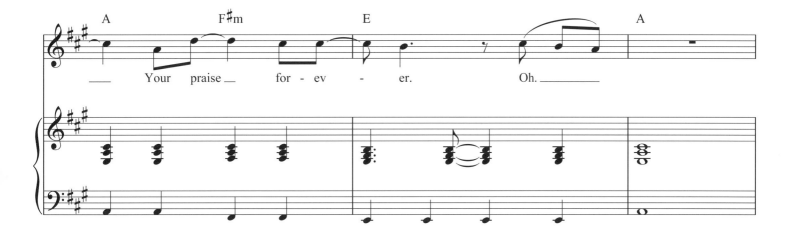

Re - mem - ber ___ love, ___

BRIDGE

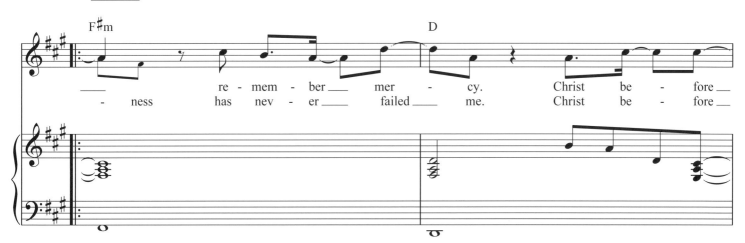

___ re - mem - ber ___ mer - cy. Christ be - fore ___
- ness has nev - er ___ failed ___ me. Christ be - fore ___

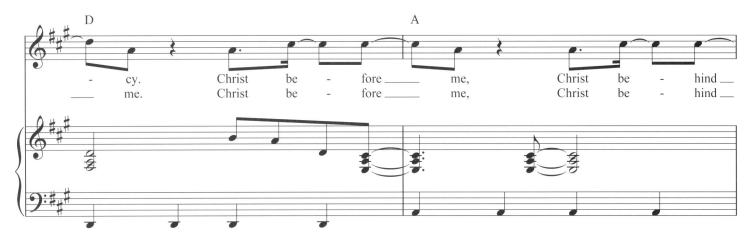

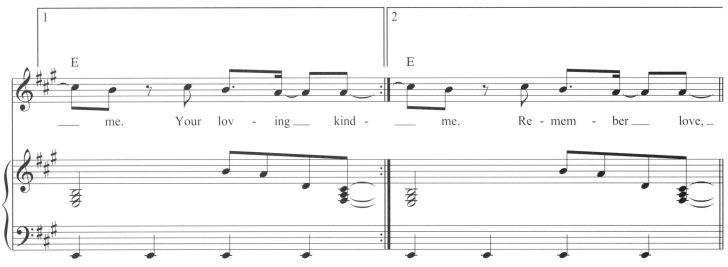

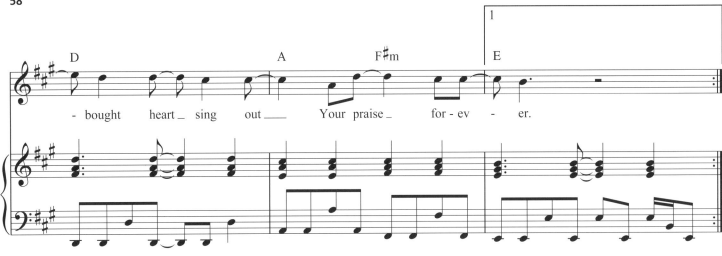

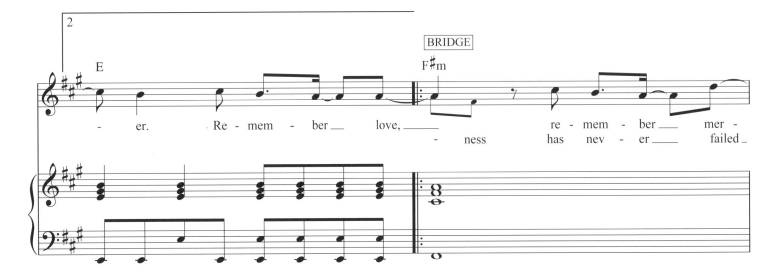

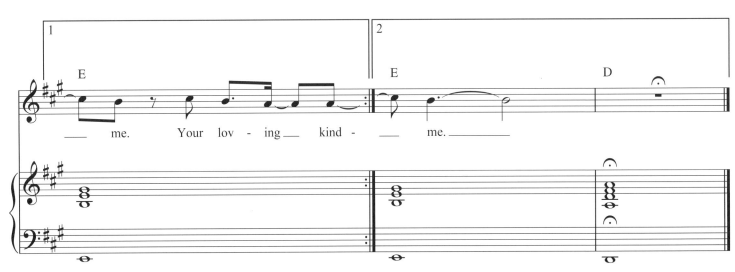

# HERE WITH YOU

Words and Music by JOSHUA GRIMMETT,
JOHANNES SHORE and JAMIE SNELL

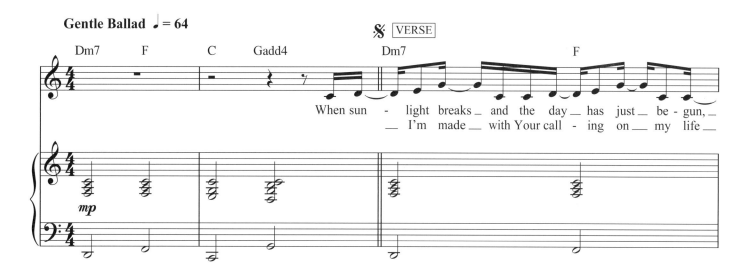

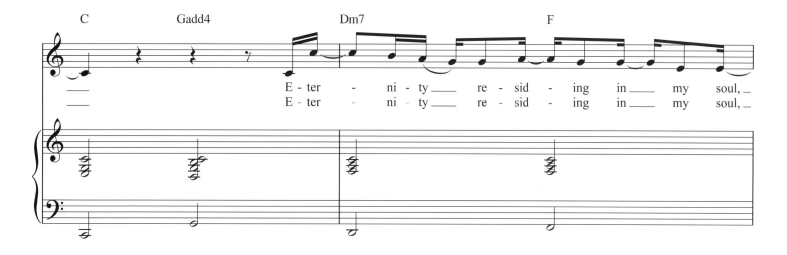

**To Coda**

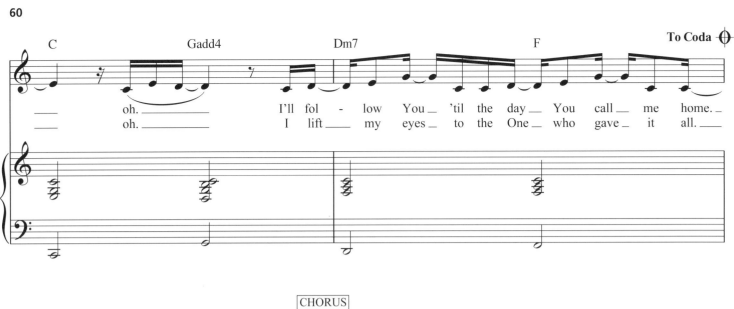

oh. _____ I'll fol - low You \_\_ 'til the day \_\_ You call \_\_ me home. \_\_
oh. _____ I lift \_\_ my eyes \_\_ to the One \_\_ who gave \_\_ it all. \_\_

CHORUS

Here now \_\_ with You, \_\_ I \_\_\_\_ have heav -

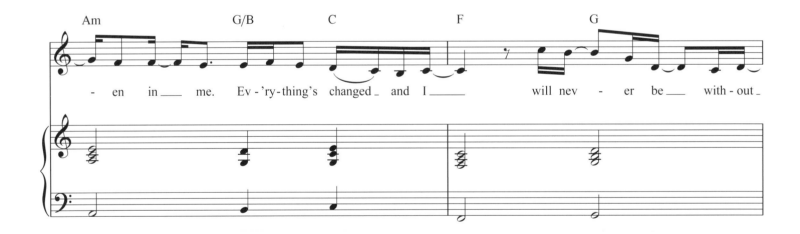

- en in \_\_ me. Ev - 'ry-thing's changed \_\_ and I \_\_\_\_ will nev - er be \_\_ with - out \_\_

**D.S. al Coda**

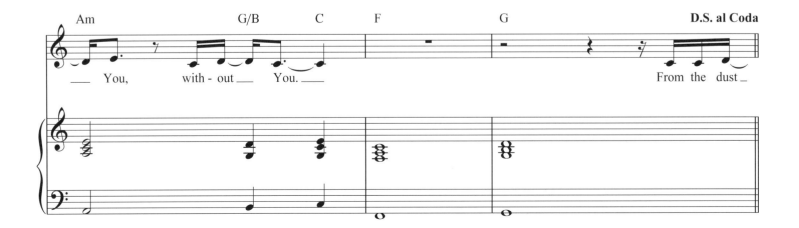

\_\_ You, with - out \_\_ You. \_\_ From the dust \_\_

**CODA**

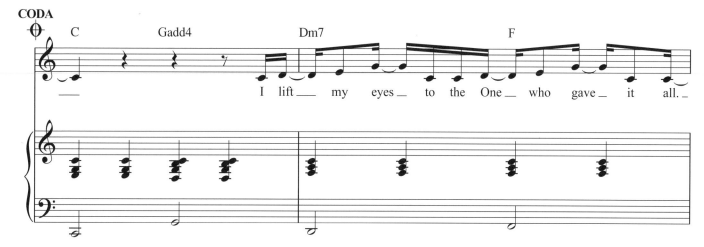

I lift __ my eyes __ to the One __ who gave __ it all. __

CHORUS

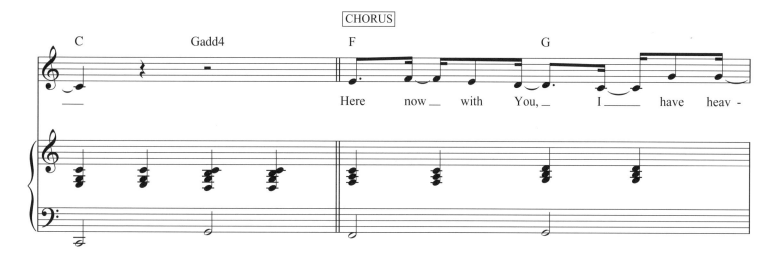

Here now __ with You, __ I _____ have heav -

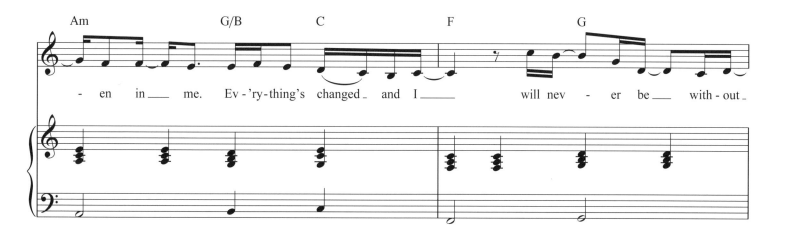

- en in ___ me. Ev -'ry-thing's changed __ and I _____ will nev - er be ___ with-out __

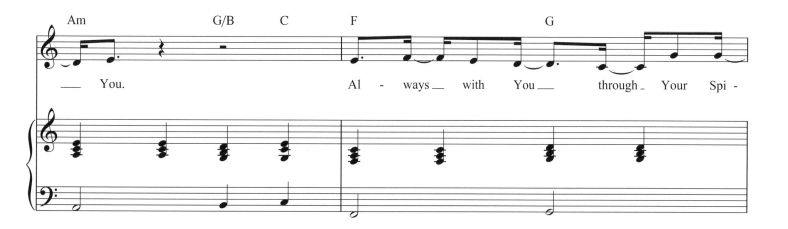

__ You. Al - ways __ with You __ through __ Your Spi -

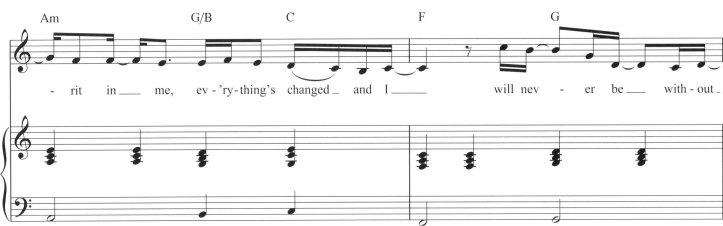

- rit in __ me, ev-'ry-thing's changed __ and I _____ will nev - er be __ with-out __

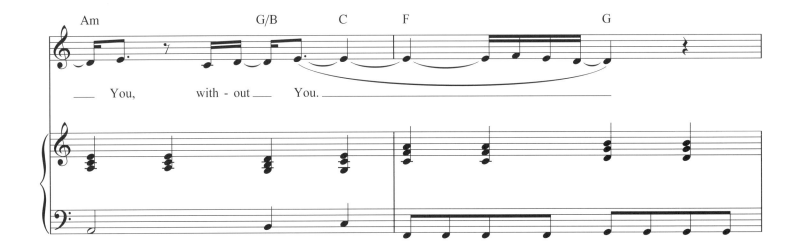

__ You, with - out __ You. _____

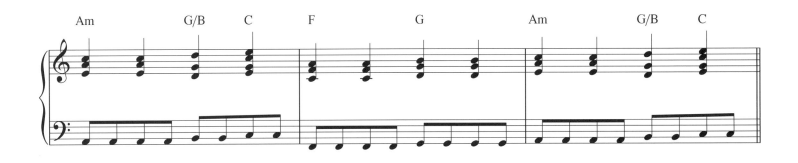

CHORUS

Here now __ with You, __ I __ have heav - en in __ me. Ev-'ry-thing's changed __ and I __

will nev - er be __ with - out __ You.

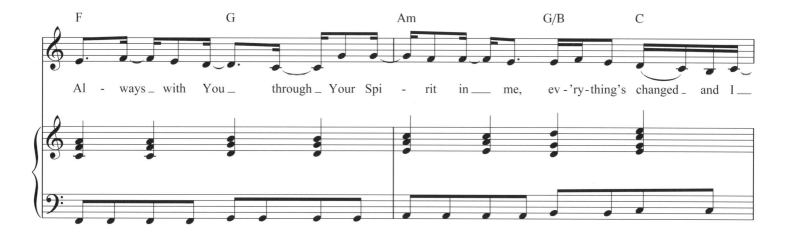

Al - ways __ with You __ through __ Your Spi - rit in __ me, ev - 'ry-thing's changed __ and I __

will nev - er be __ with - out __ You. __ You see me in the

CHORUS

fire, reach-ing out with o - pen __ hands. __ You find me on my __

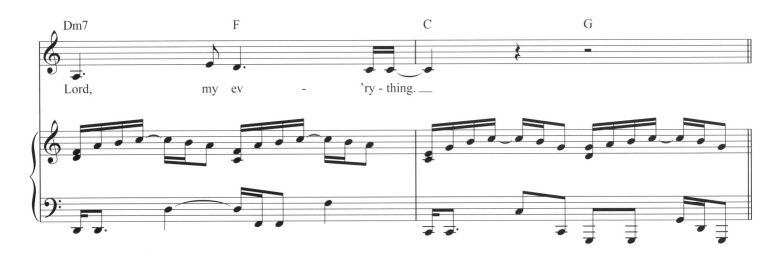

# IN GOD WE TRUST

Words and Music by REUBEN MORGAN,
BEN FIELDING and ERIC LILJERO

**With movement** ♩ = 81

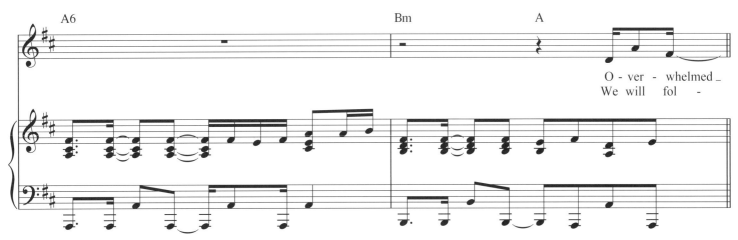

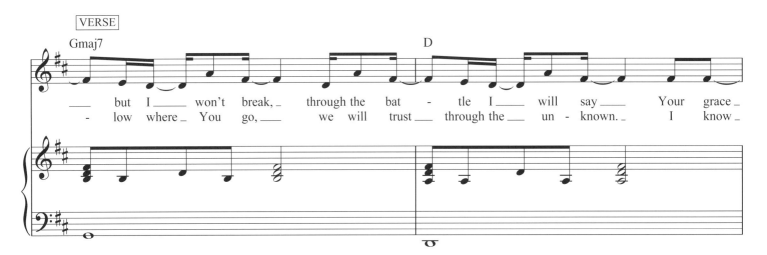

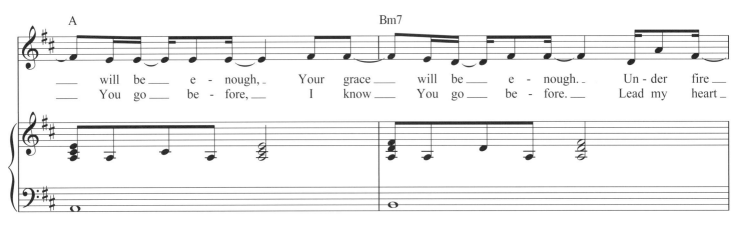

but we won't fall, ___ we will nev - er be ___ a - lone. You'll al -
now in ___ Your ways, ___ for we're car - ry - ing ___ Your Name. Your prom -

*(sing cues on repeat)*

- ways be ___ e - nough, ___ You'll al - ways be ___ e - nough. ___ } Now in
- ise nev - er fails, ___ your prom - ise nev - er fails. ___ }

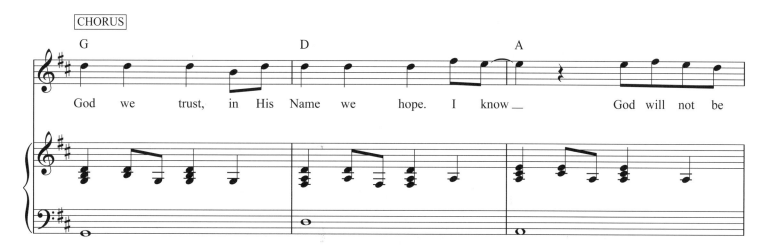

CHORUS

God we trust, in His Name we hope. I know ___ God will not be

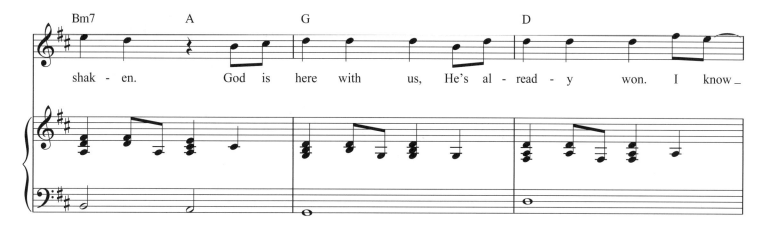

shak - en. God is here with us, He's al - read - y won. I know ___

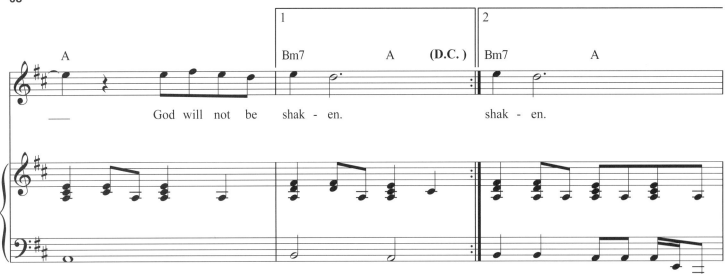

God will not be shak - en. shak - en.

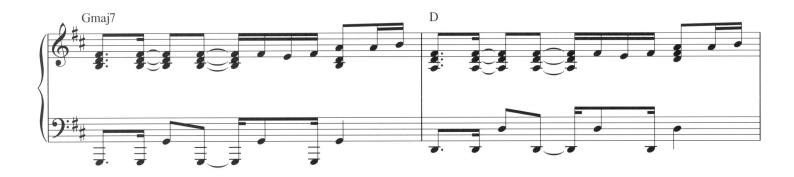

BRIDGE

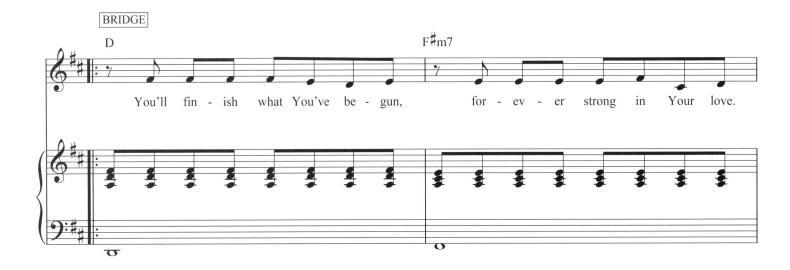

You'll fin - ish what You've be - gun, for - ev - er strong in Your love.

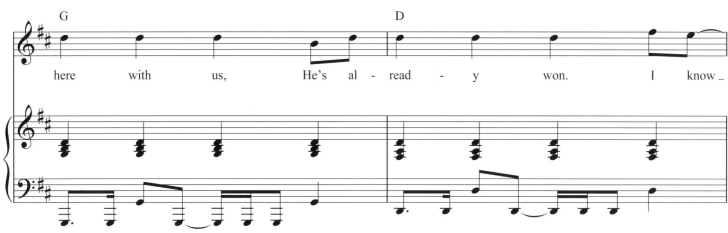

here with us, He's al - read - y won. I know _

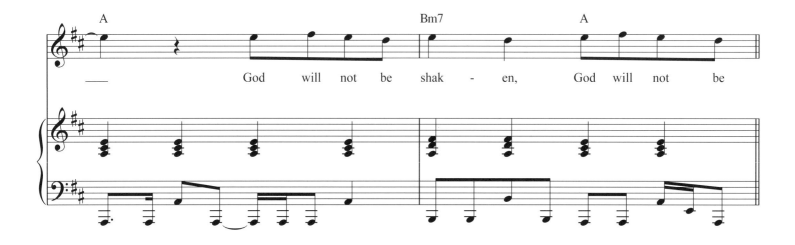

_ God will not be shak - en, God will not be

shak - en.

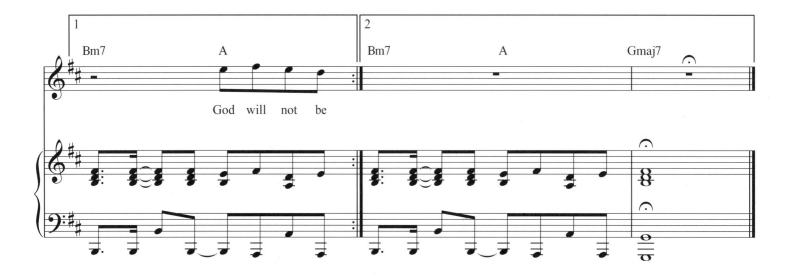

God will not be

# FAITHFULNESS

Words and Music by
CHRIS DAVENPORT

Moderate Ballad ♩ = 74

VERSE

From ris - ing __ sun 'til King-dom come,
When bat - tle's __ near, I will not fear.

Your faith - ful love is un - fail - ing.
Your prom - is - es are un - shak - en.

Though shad - ows __ turn
My faith is ___ sure

and temp - ests stir, still You, O God, are un - chang - ing.
of noth - ing more than Christ a - lone, my por - tion.

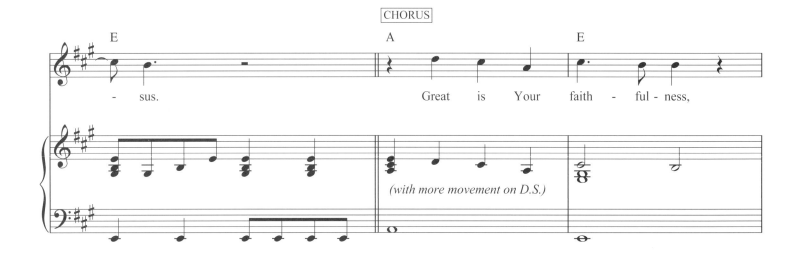

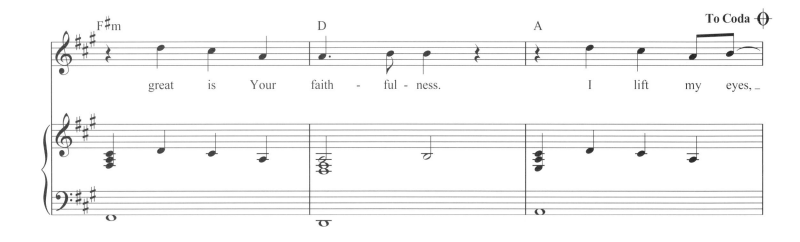

D.S. al Coda

I won't for - get _____ how great Your faith -

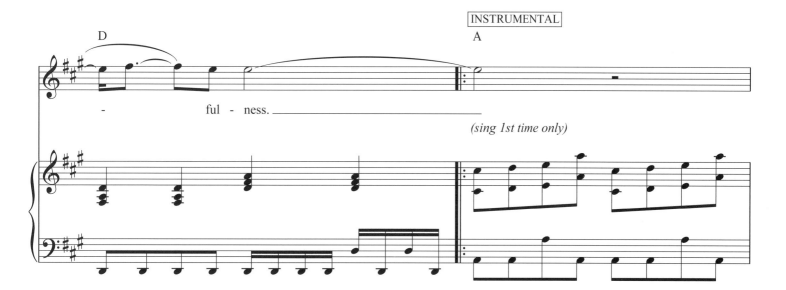

- ful - ness. _____

*(sing 1st time only)*

INSTRUMENTAL

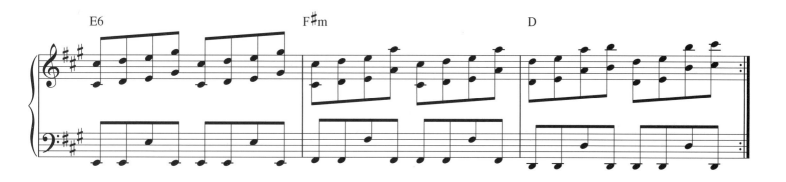

BRIDGE

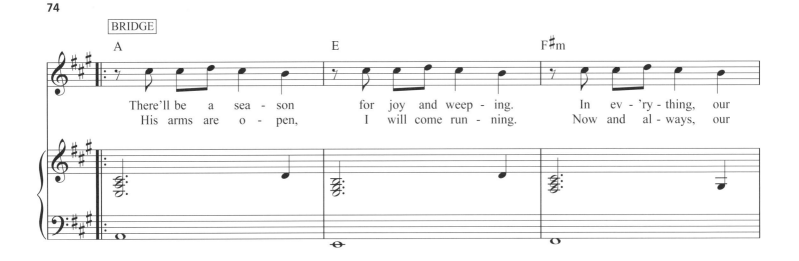

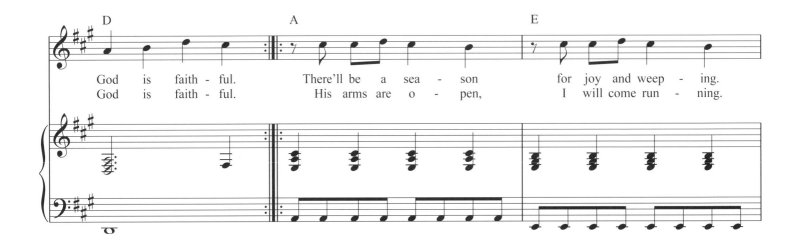

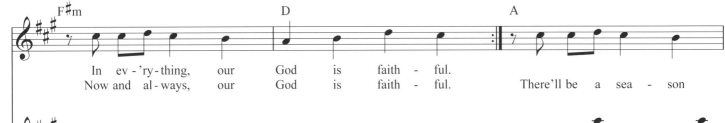

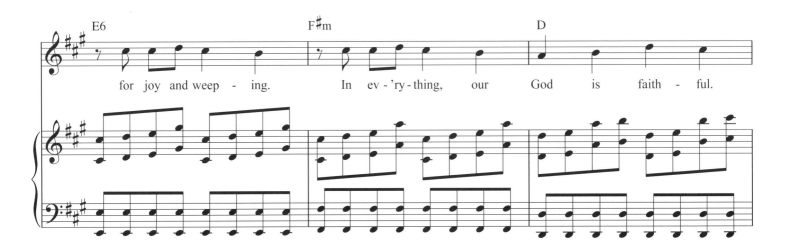

His arms are o - pen, I will come run - ning. Now and al - ways, our

CHORUS

God is faith - ful. Great is Your faith - ful - ness,

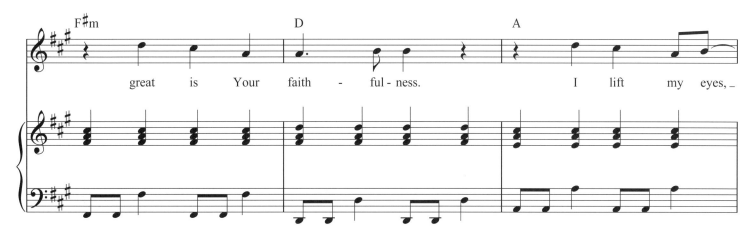

great is Your faith - ful - ness. I lift my eyes, _

1.

____ I won't for - get ____ how great Your faith - ful - ness. _____

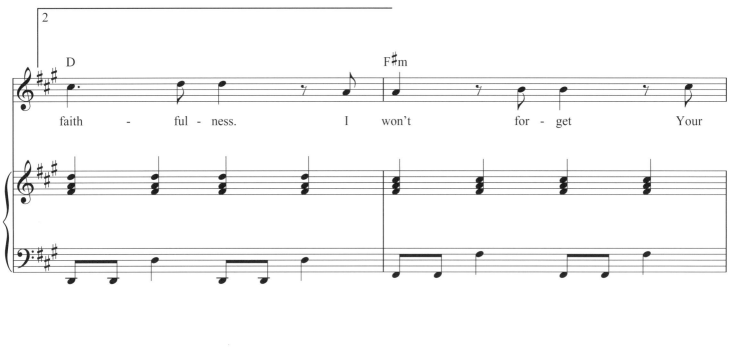

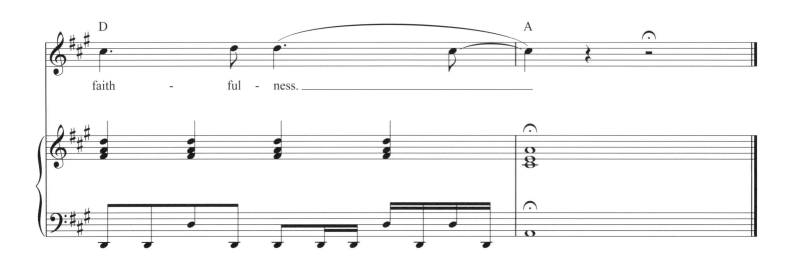

# NEVER FORSAKEN

Words and Music by BENJAMIN HASTINGS
and HANNAH HOBBS

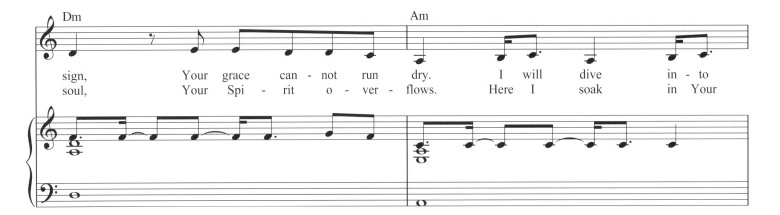

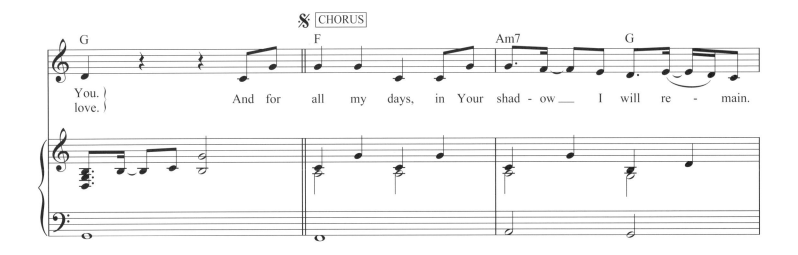

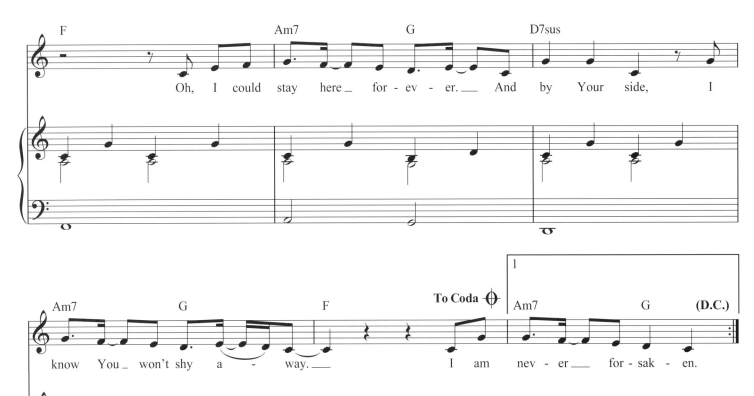

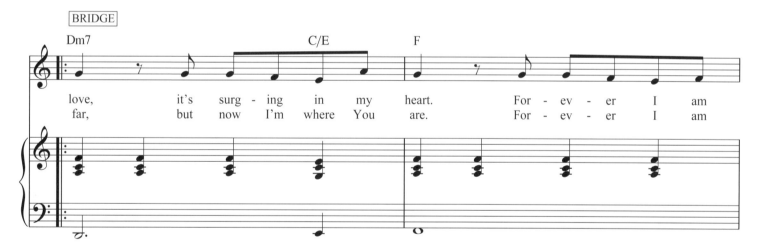

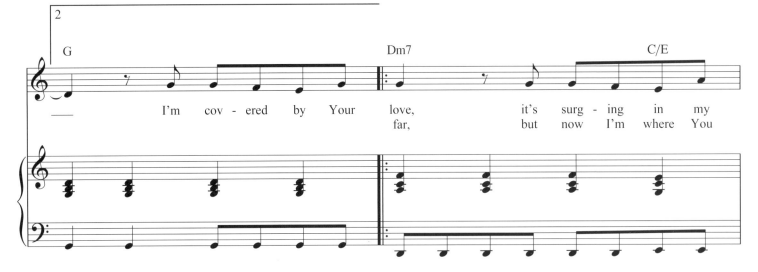

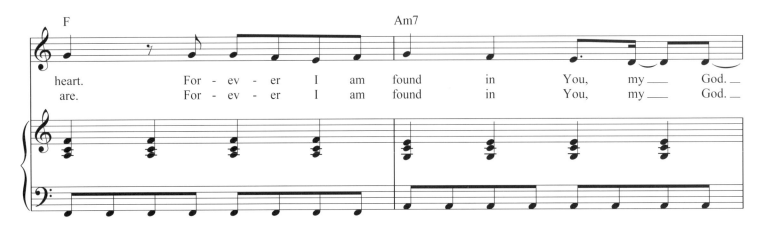

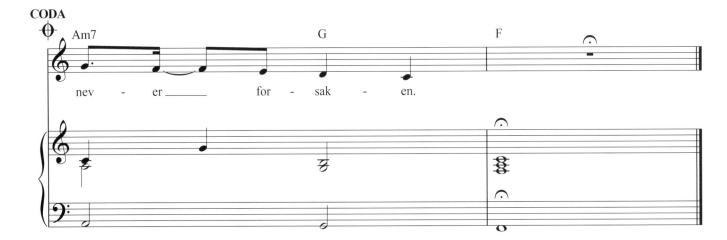